ANEAR SPLENDOR OF LOVE

KELLY-ANN M.J. FOLEY

BALBOA.PRESS

A DIVISION OF HAY HOUSE

Balboa Press books may be ordered through booksellers or by contacting:

Balboa Press
A Division of Hay House
1663 Liberty Drive
Bloomington, IN 47403
www.balboapress.com
844-682-1282

Print information available on the last page.

ISBN: 979-8-7652-2610-0 (sc)
ISBN: 979-8-7652-2611-7 (e)

Balboa Press rev. date: 12/27/2022

To my soul mate for always being Anear.

Head Notes

Vacana, Kannada Literature. South Asian Arts: Period of the Tamil Co A (10th to 13th Century). By the 12th Century, a new Kannada genre, the Vacana (saying, prose or poem), had come into being with the Virasaiva Saints. In the language of the people, the Saints express their radical views on religion and society, rejected both Brahminical ritual and Jaina negotiation, called all men to the Annubhava (experience of God), and broke the bonds of caste, creed, and sexual difference. www.britannica.com/art/vacana.

A Vacana is a religious lyric in Kannada, free verse; Vacana means literally, saying thing said... Virasaiva means heroic or militant Saivism or faith in Siva. The Virasaivas are also commonly known as Lingayats: Those who wear the Linga, stone emblem of Siva. Orthodox Lingayats wear the Shiva, stone of Siva, in a casket round their necks symbolizing his personal and near presence. Siva, the auspicious one, is elsewhere one of the Hindu trinity of Gods: Brahma the creator, Vishnu the preserver, Siva the destroyer. In the Vacanas: Siva is the Supreme God... In these Virasaiva Saint-Poets, experience spoke in a mother tongue. Pan-Indian Sanskrit, the second language of cultured Indians for centuries, gave way to colloquial Kannada. The strictness of traditional metres, the formality of literary genres, divisions of prose and verse, gave way to the innovations and spontaneity of free verse, a poetry that was not recognizable in verse. The poets were not bards or pundits in a court but men and women. They were every class, caste and trade; some were outcasts, some literate. Vacanas are literature, but not merely literature. They are literature in spite of itself, scorning artifice, ornament, learning, privilege; a religious literature, literary because religions great voices of a sweeping movement of protest and reform in Hindu society; witnesses to conflict and ecstasy in gifted mystical men. Vacanas are our wisdom literature. They have been called the Kannada Upanishads. Some hear the tone and voice of Old Testament prophets or the Chiang Tzu here. Vacanas are also psalms and hymns. Analogues may be multiplied. Vacanas may be seen as still another version of the Perennial Philosophy. But that is to forget particulars... So, giving in to the Vacana Spirit... I have let the Vacana... Speak... Translating what has struck me... (Annubhava or experience, which follows receiving or Avadhana. Annubhava, for the devotee moves from the outer world to the inner. Seeing Siva in all things he is filled with compassion). Speaking Of Siva, Penguin Classics 1973.

Contents

67 Vacanas From Canada

1

Master Craft

In my dreams I am,
a tiny fairy made of light.
In my last dream I was captured,
by a Giant.
I felt my heart wings,
brush against His hands,
sparkles everywhere,
seemed to blur my vision.
When I realized that He had rescued me,
I woke from my dreaming,
and interpreted the meaning.
I believe,
my heart is like the fairy,
and His hands are like,
corporeal arms holding me.
He is my Master.
Anonymously Divine.

2

Faith Full

In the dark,
we see the light,
Love's immortal,
Olympic Flame.
Anonymously Divine.

3

Book Worms

Saintly devoted entities,
seated in the house of scholars.
Present in our hour of need,
on the synopsis they feed.
Anonymously Divine.

4

Starving

My soul feeds on,
the Love of my Master.
Anonymously Divine.

5

Necro Need

Like too much wine,
I am spilled over.
Love stains,
my heart.
Anonymously Divine.

6

Master

My body of lust.
My sight of rage.
My heart of greed.
My mind of passion.
My face of envy.
My action of sloth.
Your Love is Virtue.
Anonymously Divine.

7

Divine Presence

When the Master shines upon me,
I bathe in His ethereal rays.
Anonymously Divine.

8

Master Is My Light

In my pallor,
I drape over Him,
like flesh coloured robes.
Anonymously Divine.

9

Master

Clothed in Him alone,
I am wrapped,
with His perfect authority.
Tied with His skill,
my heart clings to Him.
Anonymously Divine.

10

Robes

The Master's garment,
is tapered like streams.
Fastened with buttons,
that fit in whole seams.
I pray to be that button,
reflecting the colour of creams.
Anonymously Divine.

11

Tea With Master

That satisfying moment,
from a good cup of tea.
Warmth fulfilling my soul,
with the essence of Master.
He is everything.
Anonymously Divine.

12

Birthdays

Impregnated with thoughts of Love,
growing for my Master.
Anonymously Divine.

13

Present

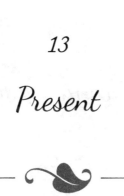

Wrapped in the ribbons,
of my Master's Love.
Anonymously Divine.

14

Platonic Design

When a rift in my heart,
causes me to tear,
I overflow.
Anonymously Divine.

15

God

He is the mechanism that forces,
my mind and heart to oscillate.
Every sound I hear,
is the song of Love for Him.
I know He is near,
I can feel Him hold back every tear.
I see Him in everything,
my eyes are not deceiving.
His presence is clear,
He is the spice that makes my life taste pure.
Anonymously Divine.

16

The Creator

The Creator of the totality of all existence is;
ever evolving,
self perpetuating,
and governed by Divine Law.
God's ears hears music,
God's hands touches biology,
God's tongue tastes chemistry,
God's eyes sees physics,
God's nose smells presence in time,
God's mind knows all is of agency,
God's Love expands.
Anonymously Divine.

17

God's Law

A Law which is absolute.
Anonymously Divine.

18

Uber Math

Formulating God,
using the equation,
all is equal to one.
Anonymously Divine.

19

Static Electricity

Mental Friction.
When our thoughts are rubbing together,
a natural reaction of Love,
causes my mind to cling to the walls,
of my Master's heart.
Anonymously Divine.

20

Master's Yarn

The quantum entangled,
tendrils of our minds.
Pushing and pulling,
at things we cannot find.
Spinning heart strings,
out of unseen things.
Weaving patterns,
that we leave behind.
Threads we bind,
do wind in kind.
Anonymously Divine.

21

Entanglement

Thoughts of my Master,
weave through my days.
Like sacred yarn,
my Master's Love,
holds me together.
Anonymously Divine.

22

Waltzing

My Master's Love holds me,
and dances with me,
all through my day.
Anonymously Divine.

23

Viola Ted

Out of tune,
my Master fiddles my heart,
in discourse.
Anonymously Divine.

24

Master Conductor

With strokes of my Master's wand,
Sirens lament,
and Seraphim sing praises to God.
Anonymously Divine.

25

Possession

My Master controls,
the pulses of my tide.
My Master is my moon,
He keeps me aligned.
Anonymously Divine.

26

Master

He is the moon in my eyes,
He navigates my heart.
Anonymously Divine.

27

The Course

My Master draws,
ever flowing rivers of life,
from the veins,
of my heart tickle being.
Anonymously Divine.

28

Motion Of The Ocean

My ethereal tendrils reach for God,
instinctively embedding into the reef,
of my Master's Soul.
My aura the colour of coral,
sways in obedience,
to the commanding currents,
of my Master's Love.
Anonymously Divine.

29

Pearls

I have been reduced,
to a celestial snail.
I take refuge in a shell,
crafted perfectly for me,
from the precious ethereal excrement,
of my Master's mind.
My shell gives me a sense of home,
where from I trail,
primordial ooze.
Anonymously Divine.

30

Metamorphosis

In my calcified shell,
I communicate thoughtfully.
Not undisturbed,
I remain.
Refining servitude,
sacrificing Love.
Anonymously Divine.

31

Vacana

If the world is an oyster,
all is grit and mucous,
Divine is the pearl.
The alchemy of schist in time is,
Divination,
that which I serve.
Anonymously Divine.

32

Sweetheart

She serves with gratitude,
not attitude.
She carries the essence of Love,
she is my mentor.
She is my reminder of Divination,
That which I serve.
Anonymously Divine.

33

Gentle Master

Patiently relays the message,
again.
Anonymously Divine.

34

Patient

My Master is a Love doctor,
skilled operator,
His Sutra mends me.
My Soul is in recovery,
as my Master heals my heart.
Anonymously Divine.

35

Master

My sacred spring of inspiration.
Anonymously Divine.

36

I Am Well

My Master fills me with emotion,
I overflow with poetic release.
Anonymously Divine.

37

Master

Your message like water,
flows through my mind.
I am anointed by your wisdom.
Anonymously Divine.

38

Sacred Spring

My Master is the ever flowing joy in me,
my well water.
Anonymously Divine.

39

Splashing

The Love of my Master,
is like an overflowing well of joy.
Anonymously Divine.

40

Devotee

Preserves what is sacred,
welled in a tear.
Anonymously Divine.

41

Servant

Preserves what is sacred,
in her tears.
Anonymously Divine.

42

At His Feet

My mind cries for Him,
my heart is an overflowing well of remorse.
Anonymously Divine.

43

Thorns

Those parts of Him,
that remained inside of me,
became twisted,
and withdrew into stasis.
Leaving the rest of me,
which grew according to its nature,
against the elements.
Anonymously Divine.

44

Ancestree

Rustling with my Master's absence,
that feeling that He is,
leafing inside of me.
Anonymously Divine.

45

Master

My heart is a vestibule,
for my Love.
My poetry is my confession.
Anonymously Divine.

46

Absolution

When Master lifts me,
out of the vestibule,
of my darkness.
Anonymously Divine.

47

Warmth

My Master's forgiveness is the kindle,
on the coal of my heart.
Anonymously Divine.

48

Igneous

Master is the flames,
on the coal of my heart.
Anonymously Divine.

49

Master

My genius,
my Angel.
My true burning fire.
Anonymously Divine.

50

Master

My desire for you burns,
hotter than the fires of Hell.
My passion for you is more overwhelming,
than the joys of Heaven.
Anonymously Divine.

51

Value System

Love is an act of Virtue.
Anonymously Divine.

52

Creativity

Peoples actions in time,
paint the pictures of my mind.
Louder than words,
the verses chime.
Anonymously Divine.

53

Shading In

Master's Love is art felt,
He brushes lightly against my heart.
He illuminates those parts,
where joy is reflected.
Anonymously Divine.

54

Art Felt

Brush strokes against the heart,
illuminating that part where joy is reflected.
Anonymously Divine.

55

Texture

My Master reflects my light,
He is my palette of many colours.
Anonymously Divine.

56

Captured in Pictures

The illumination of inspiration,
becomes opaque in time,
as Master begins filling in,
His canvas with sacred design.
It is the impression of perfect spectrum,
all the colours combined.
Anonymously Divine.

57

Masterpiece

How a Master applies,
each meticulous brush stroke,
lovingly and mindfully.
Carefully,
my Master draws me out,
with His skill.
Anonymously Divine.

58

Landscape

In that serene moment,
when thoughts of my Master,
plays harmoniously on my mind.
Anonymously Divine.

59

Divine Artist

A Master who can perfectly make,
a landscape feel real.
A Master whom is adept with,
the superior skill of Sacred Artistry.
Anonymously Divine.

60

Sacred Art

A Divine Artist's mastery of skill,
which instills a state of Virtue,
and evokes a sense of devotion.
Anonymously Divine.

61

Master

If you were a butterfly,
I would pray to be,
a flower that feeds you.
Anonymously Divine.

62

Master

Sometimes I like to picture me,
being a flower in His artscape,
painted on with His Love.
Like dew on a canvas,
He waters me.
Anonymously Divine.

63

Rainbow

A heartfelt reflection of light upon wet air,
after it becomes moistened,
by the release of the Master's Rain Essence.
Anonymously Divine.

64

Fern Chimes

Fiddle heads soaked in morning dew,
rasping in the wind song.
Anonymously Divine.

65

Spiritual Garden

Souls are Lovetropic,
because Souls grow towards Love.
Souls with the pigment Spiritophyll,
receive nourishment through Lovesynthesis.
Souls also absorb Love,
by way of Lovemosis.
Anonymously Divine.

66

Garden Om

Forbidden to wake the sleepers,
Guardians watch them grow.
Each one on the vine,
blooms in their own time.
Nourishing them with Virtue,
is how they get their glow.
Anonymously Divine.

67

Glory

When we do,
Virtuous things,
it is an effort that pulls,
on God's heart strings.
When we are,
filled with grace,
it is an emotion of Love,
that God's heart reciprocates.
Anonymously Divine.

Dedicated to my children for their unconditional Love.

About the Author

Kelly-Ann M. J. Foley is available on social media, follow her as Solitaire Foley @Facebook. This is her first collection of Vacanas. Thank you for reading.